# POCKET COMMEMORATION BOOK

with lists for the living and departed

Copyright © 2019 Exaltation Press

"Pocket Commemoration Book"

This book is designed as an aid for Orthodox Christians to help them keep track of who they should be praying for. While it is not a prayer book, it is designed to go along with morning and evening prayers as a supplement.

All rights reserved. This book or any portion thereof may not be reproduced or used in any manner whatsoever without the express written permission of the publisher except for the use of brief quotations in a book review.

ISBN: 978-1-950067-49-7 (Paperback)

First printing edition 2019

Exaltation Press
Grand Rapids, MI

www.ExaltationPress.com

For bulk orders, please contact editor@exaltationpress.com

# TABLE OF CONTENTS

**INTRODUCTION** 5

**THE LIVING** 7
- MY FAMILY 8
- MY SPIRITUAL FAMILY 10
- THE CLERGY 11
- FELLOW PARISHIONERS 12
- THE CIVIL AUTHORITIES 14
- THE SICK 16
- THE POOR, HUNGRY, AND THOSE IN FINANCIAL HARDSHIPS 18
- EXPECTANT MOTHERS AND THEIR UNBORN CHILDREN 19
- THOSE DESIRING TO CONCEIVE 20
- THOSE DESIRING MARRIAGE 21
- THOSE IN MOURNING 22
- THOSE IN DIFFICULT CIRCUMSTANCES 23
- THOSE WHO HAVE WRONGED US OR WHOM WE HAVE WRONGED AND FOR RECONCILIATION 24
- PERSONAL LISTS 25
- OTHER LIVING 28
- OTHER NON-ORTHODOX LIVING 30

**THE DEPARTED** 32
- MY FAMILY WHO HAVE FALLEN ASLEEP 33
- SPIRITUAL FAMILY WHO HAVE FALLEN ASLEEP 35
- THE CLERGY 36
- DEPARTED PARISHIONERS 37
- ALL CHILDREN LOST IN THE WOMB 38
- THOSE WHO WRONGED US OR WHOM WE WRONGED AND DID NOT RECONCILE WITH IN THIS LIFE 40
- OTHER DEPARTED 42
- OTHER NON-ORTHODOX DEPARTED 44

# INTRODUCTION

*"Continue steadfastly in prayer, being watchful in it with thanksgiving."* - Col. 4:2

Prayer is the arena in which we live out our life in Christ. It is the beginning of all the virtues. The prayers that we offer, however, are not only for ourselves. As Orthodox Christians, members of the Body of Christ, we are called to pray for each other and for the life of the world around us. That prayer, the prayer of the Church, is a powerful thing. Although God does not need our prayers, in His mercy, He wills to work through the prayers of those who love Him.

But how often do we forget to pray for those in need? How often when someone asks us to pray for them, do we tell them that we will and then forget? In the Old Testament, the Prophet Samuel showed us how serious that is when he said, *"Far be it from me that I should sin against the Lord by ceasing to pray for you!"* (1 Sam. 12:23)

To avoid that, to make sure that we pray for others, from early on Christians have kept lists of names of those needing prayer, lists of both the living and the dead. The Church has lists like these which are called the diptychs. Individual Orthodox Christians and families likewise keep their own personal lists, where they remember their families, friends, loved ones, and anyone else in need of prayer.

This book, kept intentionally simple, is to be used for keeping track of your own or your family's diptychs. Update it as often as you can. Write names in pencil. When someone asks you to pray for them, do not promise that you will and then forget. Rather, say a prayer for them as soon as they ask and then add their name to this book.

When you pray, pray to the merciful Lord with zeal and faith and always remember to follow up, if possible, with those for whom you are praying. That way, you can be sure you are praying for their current needs and can rejoice in the mercy the Lord shows them.

And never forget to pray for the dead. When we pray for them, offering their souls up to Christ, we show love for them, just as we know in faith that the departed in Christ pray for us. That bond of love - prayer - unites us all in Christ.

# THE LIVING

Although we should pray for the whole world in general and for anyone who asks for our prayers, God has placed each of us in particular families and parishes and given each of us particular people for whom it is especially important for us to pray: our family members (parents, spouses, children, and other family), our godparents and godchildren, our clergy, the leaders of the land we live in, our particular friends and enemies.

Also, not everyone has the same needs. Some need prayers for healing, others need prayers for help in difficult financial circumstances, still others need prayers for a successful pregnancy.

In the pages that follow, write in the names of all of those who need your prayers, according to the individual need of each.

At the end of this section, there are some additional pages where you can write in more names of the living or lists of those with a particular need not mentioned elsewhere.

Begin by making the Sign of the Cross and saying, "Save, O Lord, and have mercy on Thy servants..."

# My Family

My Spouse: _____

My Parents and Grandparents:

_____

_____

My Spouse's Parents: _____

My Children:

_____

_____

_____

_____

Other Relatives, Among the Living:

_____

_____

Non-Orthodox Relatives:

# My Spiritual Family

My Godparent(s): _____

My Godchildren:

_____

_____

_____

_____

_____

Others:

_____

_____

_____

_____

_____

# The Clergy

*"Obey your leaders and submit to them, for they are keeping watch over your souls, as those who will have to give an account. Let them do this with joy and not with groaning, for that would be of no advantage to you."* - Heb. 13:17

My Bishops (Patriarch, Metropolitan, Bishop, etc):

_____

My Spiritual Father: _____

Other Clergy and Monastics:

_____

_____

_____

_____

_____

_____

# Fellow Parishioners

# The Civil Authorities

*"First of all, then, I urge that supplications, prayers, intercessions, and thanksgivings be made for all people, for kings and all who are in high positions, that we may lead a peaceful and quiet life, godly and dignified in every way."* - 1 Tim. 2:1-2

The Head of State: _____

The Legislature and the Courts

The Governor of the State/Province Where I Live:

_____

The Mayor and All Other Local Officials:

_____

Those Who Protect Us: Police, Firefighters, Medical Professionals, and All Other Local People Who Serve, Especially:

_____

_____

Those Serving in the Armed Forces, for the Safety of Their Souls and Bodies:

_____

_____

_____

_____

_____

All Others in Authority, That the Lord Would Give Them Wisdom and a Blameless Conscience:

_____

_____

_____

_____

_____

# The Sick

*"O All-Merciful God: Father, Son, and Holy Spirit, O Undivided Trinity, who art worshipped and glorified, look graciously on Thy servants who are ill, grant them remission of all their sins and healing from their diseases. Give them health and physical strength, length of days and a prosperous life, and the enjoyment of Thy blessings in peace, so that they, together with us, may offer prayers of thanksgiving unto Thee, our most gracious God and Creator."* - Prayer for the Healing of the Sick

_____

_____

_____

_____

_____

_____

_____

## The Poor, Hungry, and Those in Financial Hardships

*"If a brother or sister is poorly clothed and lacking in daily food, and one of you says to them, 'Go in peace, be warmed and filled,' without giving them the things needed for the body, what good is that?"*
- James 2:15-17

_____

_____

_____

_____

_____

_____

_____

_____

_____

# Expectant Mothers and Their Unborn Children

Through His incarnation, our Lord Jesus Christ sanctified His Mother's womb and made motherhood itself holy and sacred. Our Lord also knows each of us even before our birth.

# Those Desiring to Conceive

*"Look down, O merciful one, on Thy servants (names) who are joined together in the bond of marriage and who are beseeching Thy help. May Thy mercy be upon them so that they may be fruitful and may see their children's children even to the third and fourth generation and may live to a good old age and enter into the Kingdom of Heaven through Thy Son, our Lord Jesus Christ, to whom be glory, honor, and worship with the Holy Spirit to the ages. Amen."* - Prayer to be Granted Children

_____

_____

_____

_____

_____

_____

_____

# Those Desiring Marriage

*"O Lord, hear my humble prayer, offered Thee from the depth of my heart, and grant Thy servant (name) an honorable and pious spouse, that together they may live in love and harmony, glorifying Thee, O Merciful God: the Father, the Son, and the Holy Spirit, now and ever and unto ages of ages. Amen."*
- Prayer for a Spouse

_____

_____

_____

_____

_____

_____

_____

_____

# Those in Mourning

# Those in Difficult Circumstances

# Those Who Have Wronged Us or Whom We Have Wronged and for Reconciliation

# Personal Lists

## Those Who _____

_____

_____

_____

_____

_____

_____

_____

_____

_____

_____

_____

_____

**Those Who** _____

# Those Who _____

## Other Living

# Other Non-Orthodox Living

# THE DEPARTED

Through the Cross, the Grave, and His glorious Resurrection on the third Day, our Lord and God Jesus Christ showed us that death is no longer something that we have to fear. By His death, He has conquered death and opened the way to Paradise for all. Prayer for the dead is a good, holy, and Christian act.

In the Old Testament, we read: *"He then took up a collection among all his soldiers, amounting to two thousand silver drachmas, which he sent to Jerusalem to provide for an expiatory sacrifice. In doing this he acted in a very excellent and noble way, inasmuch as he had the resurrection in mind; for if he were not expecting the fallen to rise again, it would have been superfluous and foolish to pray for the dead. But if he did this with a view to the splendid reward that awaits those who had gone to rest in godliness, it was a holy and pious thought. Thus he made atonement for the dead that they might be absolved from their sin."* - 2 Maccabees 12:43-46

Begin by making the Sign of the Cross and saying, "Give rest, O Lord, to the soul of Thy servants..."

# My Family Who Have Fallen Asleep

My Spouse: _____

My Parents and Grandparents:

_____

_____

My Spouse's Parents: _____

My Children:

_____

_____

_____

_____

Other Relatives, Among the Departed:

_____

_____

Non-Orthodox Relatives:

# Spiritual Family Who Have Fallen Asleep

My Godparent(s): _____

My Godchildren:

_____

_____

_____

_____

_____

Others:

_____

_____

_____

_____

_____

# The Clergy

Past Bishops Who Have Reposed in Christ

_____

Past Spiritual Fathers: _____

The Priest Who Baptized Me: _____

Other Clergy and Monastics:

_____

_____

_____

_____

_____

_____

_____

# Departed Parishioners

# All Children Lost in the Womb

Although these children were not able to receive the washing of Holy Baptism, as Christians we know that God knows each of us from our mother's womb and so we pray for all children who died from miscarriage or other causes and commend them into the arms of our loving God and Savior. It is good and proper that such children be given names, if possible, in recognition of their personhood, as created in the Image and Likeness of God. God does not forget about a single one of His creatures.

_____

_____

_____

_____

_____

_____

# Those Who Wronged Us or Whom We Wronged and Did Not Reconcile With in This Life

_____

_____

_____

_____

_____

_____

_____

_____

_____

_____

_____

# Other Departed

# Other Non-Orthodox Departed

THE END. ALL GLORY BE TO GOD.

www.ingramcontent.com/pod-product-compliance
Lightning Source LLC
Chambersburg PA
CBHW030135100526
44591CB00009B/665